TOMOKO NINOMIYA

TRANSLATED AND ADAPTED BY
David and Eriko Walsh

LETTERED BY
Michaelis/Carpelis Design

BALLANTINE BOOKS • NEW YORK

A Del Rey Books Trade Paperback Original

Published in the United States by Del Rey Books, an imprint of The Random House Publishing Group, a division of Random House, Inc., New York.

First published in Japan in 2002 by Kodansha Ltd., Tokyo.

Library of Congress Catalog Control Number: 2005921798

ISBN 0-345-48173-9

Printed in the United States of America

www.delreymanga.com

9 8 7 6 5 4 3 2 1

Lettering—Michaelis/Carpelis Design Associates Inc.

Contents

A Note from the Author
iv

Honorifics Explained
v

Lesson 7
5

Lesson 8
33

Lesson 9
61

Lesson 10
91

Lesson 11
119

Lesson 12
148

Special Thanks
179

Translation Notes
181

Preview of Volume 3
186

A Note from the Author

I had originally started out writing
a comic about youth involved in classical
music, but now it seems the characters
are getting a little odd...
I can't say where this is going... My apologies.
Tomoko Ninomiya

Honorifics Explained

Throughout the Del Rey Manga books, you will find Japanese honorifics left intact in the translations. For those not familiar with how the Japanese use honorifics and, more important, how they differ from American honorifics, we present this brief overview.

Politeness has always been a critical facet of Japanese culture. Ever since the feudal era, when Japan was a highly stratified society, use of honorifics—which can be defined as polite speech that indicates relationship or status—has played an essential role in the Japanese language. When addressing someone in Japanese, an honorific usually takes the form of a suffix attached to one's name (example: "Asuna-san"), or as a title at the end of one's name or in place of the name itself (example: "Negi-sensei," or simply "Sensei!").

Honorifics can be expressions of respect or endearment. In the context of manga and anime, honorifics give insight into the nature of the relationship between characters. Many translations into English leave out these important honorifics, and therefore distort the "feel" of the original Japanese. Because Japanese honorifics contain nuances that English honorifics lack, it is our policy at Del Rey not to translate them. Here, instead, is a guide to some of the honorifics you may encounter in Del Rey Manga.

-san: This is the most common honorific and is equivalent to Mr., Miss, Ms., or Mrs. It is the all-purpose honorific and can be used in any situation where politeness is required.

-sama: This is one level higher than "-san" and is used to confer great respect.

-dono: This comes from the word "tono," which means "lord." It is an even higher level than "-sama" and confers utmost respect.

-kun: This suffix is used at the end of boys' names to express familiarity or endearment. It is also sometimes used by men among friends, or when addressing someone younger or of a lower station.

-chan: This is used to express endearment, mostly toward girls. It is also used for little boys, pets, and even among lovers. It gives a sense of childish cuteness.

Bozu: This is an informal way to refer to a boy, similar to the English term "kid" or "squirt."

Sempai: This title suggests that the addressee is one's senior in a group or organization. It is most often used in a school setting, where underclassmen refer to their upperclassmen as "sempai." It can also be used in the workplace, such as when a newer employee addresses an employee who has seniority in the company.

Kohai: This is the opposite of "sempai" and is used toward underclassmen in school or newcomers in the workplace. It connotes that the addressee is of a lower station.

Sensei: Literally meaning "one who has come before," this title is used for teachers, doctors, or masters of any profession or art.

[blank]: Usually forgotten in these lists, but perhaps the most significant difference between Japanese and English. The lack of honorific means that the speaker has permission to address the person in a very intimate way. Usually, only family, spouses, or very close friends have this kind of permission. Known as *yobisute,* it can be gratifying when someone who has earned the intimacy starts to call one by one's name without an honorific. But when that intimacy hasn't been earned, it can be very insulting.

のだめ カンタービレ
Nodame Cantabile
#2
二ノ宮知子
TOMOKO NINOMIYA

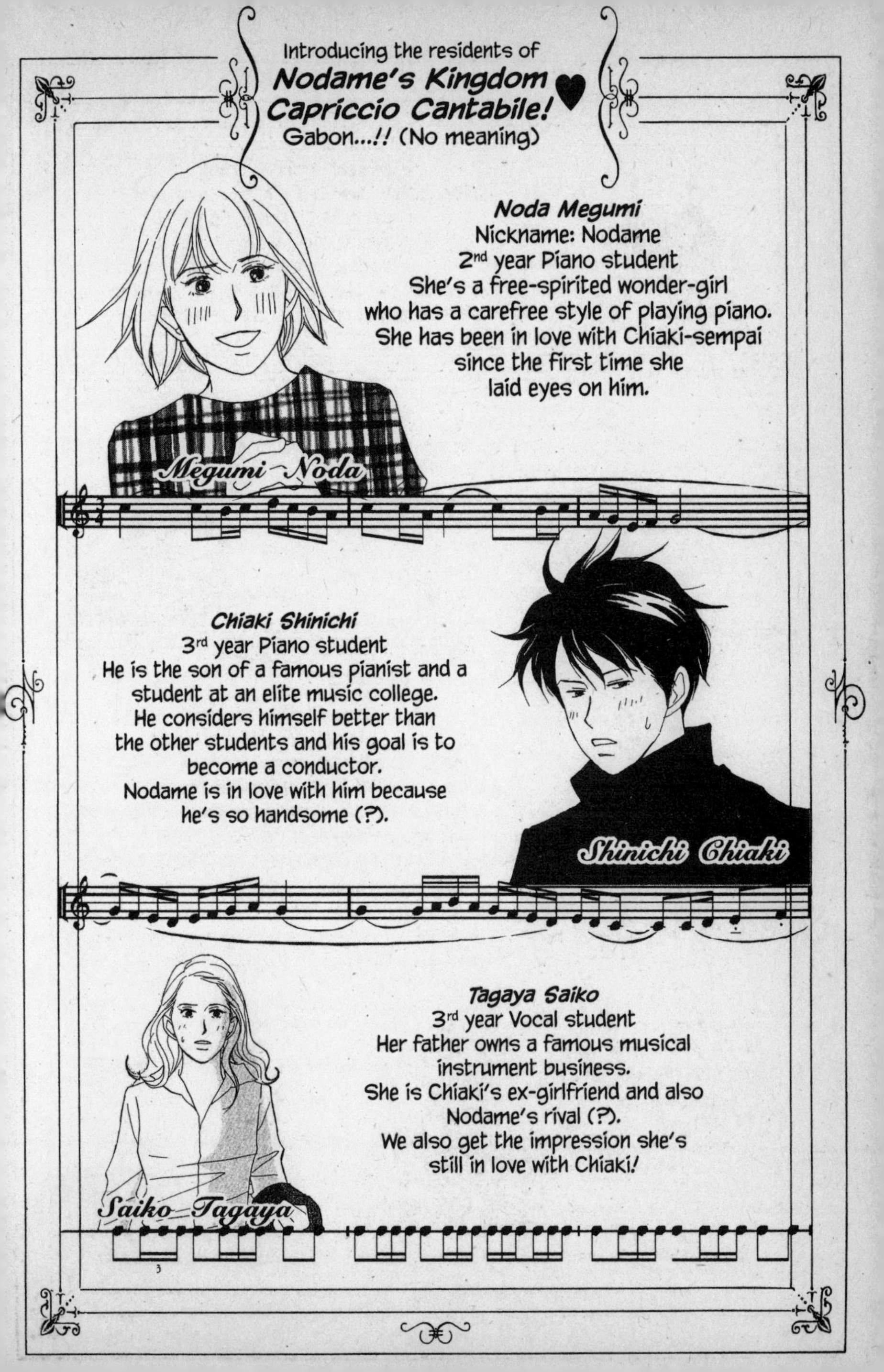
Introducing the residents of
Nodame's Kingdom
Capriccio Cantabile! ♥
Gabon...!! (No meaning)
Noda Megumi
Nickname: Nodame
2nd year Piano student
She's a free-spirited wonder-girl
who has a carefree style of playing piano.
She has been in love with Chiaki-sempai
since the first time she
laid eyes on him.
Megumi Noda
Chiaki Shinichi
3rd year Piano student
He is the son of a famous pianist and a
student at an elite music college.
He considers himself better than
the other students and his goal is to
become a conductor.
Nodame is in love with him because
he's so handsome (?).
Shinichi Chiaki
Tagaya Saiko
3rd year Vocal student
Her father owns a famous musical
instrument business.
She is Chiaki's ex-girlfriend and also
Nodame's rival (?).
We also get the impression she's
still in love with Chiaki!
Saiko Tagaya

Mine Ryutaro
2nd year Violin student
His father owns a Chinese restaurant
right next to the college.
He plays electric violin and is a
rocker boy at heart.
In many ways Nodame and he have similar
personalities, and they are also friends!
Ryutaro Mine
Okuyama Masumi
3rd year Orchestral Music student
He's claustrophobic and is a timpanist.
Okuyama is also in love with Chiaki.
He's a girl (?) and considers
Nodame his rival.
No! No! Okuyama is a boy
with a mustache! ♥
Masumi Okuyama
Franz von Stresemann
(also calls himself Milch Holstein)
He's an old man from Germany
who calls himself just an honest tourist.
But the real truth is he's a world-famous conductor.
However, he seems more like a dirty
old man who's trying to sexually harass Nodame.
Franz von Stresemann
Sebastiano Viera
He's the world-renowned
conductor whom Chiaki
respects the most.
Chiaki's dream is to
become a conductor
like him!
Sebastiano Viera
—Other professors at the college—
Eto Kouzo
The "elite specialist harisen-sensei."
Tanioka Hajime
Teacher who is the
"struggling student" specialist.

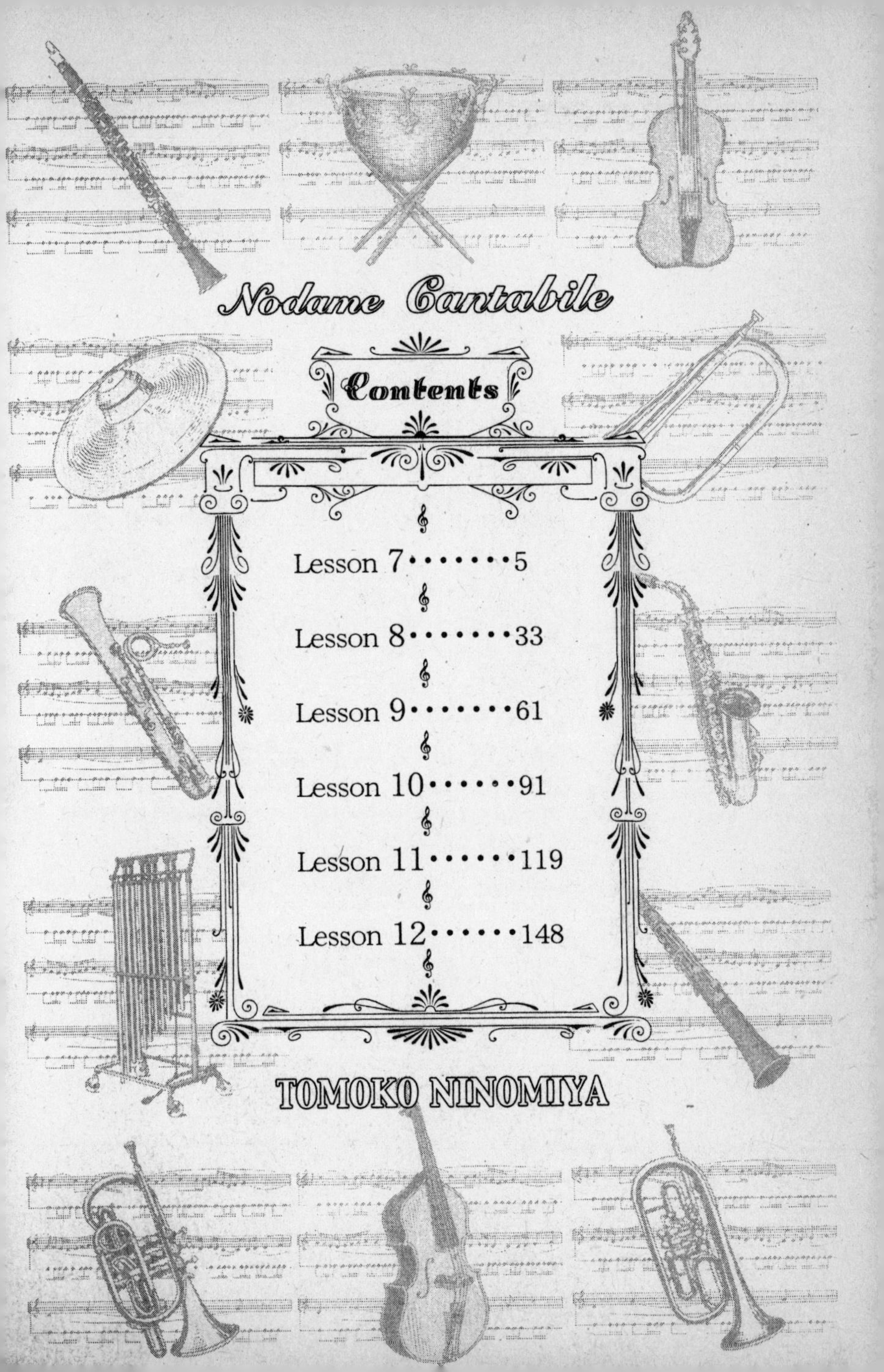

Nodame Cantabile

Contents

Lesson 7 5

Lesson 8 33

Lesson 9 61

Lesson 10 91

Lesson 11 119

Lesson 12 148

TOMOKO NINOMIYA

Lesson 7

Momongaoka Music Academy
Momongaoka Music Graduate School
Momongaoka Music University
Tempo 120
DUM DUM
126...
DUM
132...
DUM DUM
DUM DUM

162...
ハァ
PANT
ハァ
PANT
ハァ
PANT
ドコドコドコドコッ
DUTA
DUTA
DUTA
DUTA
FOOSH
No...!!
No more!
I can't stand it!!
わーっ
WAA HH

Wha...? What was that all about?
Oh, that's just Masumi-chan.
HA HA HA
She has claustrophobia. It freaks her out being in the practice rooms.
It always happens.
But she's a really good timpanist.
She's in the A orchestra.
Marimbas, drums...
She considers herself the "Queen of percussion"!
"She" ...?
"Queen" ...?
No more!
I wanna go home to Yamagata!!

I want to go back to live under Yamagata's big sky!
AH HA HA
But...
Hey...
There's Chiaki-sama!
Oh, yeah!
Chiaki-sama!?
Ah...
But because Chiaki-sama is here in Tokyo... I can't leave this school.
So cool...

Just one time I'd like the chance to talk to Chiaki-sama.
Chiaki-sempai!!
Eh!
Thanks for waiting. ♡
I wasn't waiting for you!
Sempai, are you going to practice?
UKYU
Why is she acting like this even at school...
Nodame wants to listen to you play piano!
Don't follow me!
You're bothering me!
Huh? Can't you be nice...
We'll always be together
Megumi Noda, 2nd year piano student

She's the number one person on my list to kill!!
She's holding his arm! Holding his arm! Holding his arm!
ザッ
SHK
ザッ
SHK
ふー
PHEW...
Ahh... that's it.

Great! Did you compose that music?!
Nice song!
ギャピー
GYAPEE
It's romantic... ♡
Romant...
You think so?
Is that because of the second movement?
OOPS
You're going to name it "Rhapsody for Nodame," right!
Don't tell me what to name my song!
キャ
SQUEAL
Back off!
I'm writing this piece for an orchestra to perform...
...and it's going to be a little louder.
An orchestra!?
IMPRESSED
Are you writing the parts for all the instruments?!
Yeah...
That's great!!
But even so, I don't have an orchestra to perform it.
The fact is, I'm still just a student.

An orchestra...
What's the matter? Don't you feel good?
Is some-thing wrong?
Oh, I know!
Don't worry, we can just make nabe for dinner tonight. ♡
WHACK
バゴー
ぎゃぼん
OWW
I guess he wasn't worried about what we were having for dinner...
SNIFFLE
But...
He asked me to buy groceries for dinner...
SHOPPING LIST
ギャピー
YIPPEE
It's like we're husband and wife!

SPLASH
KUNG
Hey, what hap-pened?
Are you OK?
A bucket of water fell on her head!
Who did that?!
Hnn...
There's no one up there.
???
SWEET HOUSE

You will die if you don't write a copy of this letter to 100 people within 2 days.
From the Death Committee.
A letter!
Is this from my mom!?
202
CHIAKI
Please help me write these letters!!
WAHH
LETTER SET
You're crazy!!
A chain letter!?
WSHICK
No one sends these anymore. This is a mischievous joke!!

Mischievous.... Who would do that!?
Who cares!
DEATH COMMITTEE...
Does someone hold a grudge against you?
There's no one that you suspect?
Thief!
Thief!
She stole her lunch 28 times.
Maki-chan...?
Or the old lady from the cafeteria at school?
The neighborhood fish market!?
What did you do....?
By the way, where are the groceries I asked you to get for supper?
Did you buy them?
Uh... yeah!
Here they are.
But... the shopping list got wet and I had trouble reading it.
LOCUSTS
ZASAI
SPRING ROLLS
These were the only things I could read...

I told you to get groceries for nabe!!
Dry tangle, nappa, shun-giku...!!
ええーっ
なべ!?
Oh yeah...!? Nabe!
Then why did you want locusts!?
Well, we can make hot locust soup....
UGHH
No way!
He hates them so much it makes him shake.
SLIP
ズベッ
OOPH
Ohh!
Banana skin....
パンパン
POP POP
WAHH!
FIRE CRACKER
ガラッ
SLIDE
ボムッ
KLUNK

WAA!
GO AWAY NODAME!
Maki-chan, I'm sorry!!
I didn't do it!!
It's an old grudge you hold, isn't it.
IDIOT
Someone close by must have done this.
I don't know who did it, but it serves you right.
HN!
I hope you've learned your lesson! No more stealing lunches!
I can't promise!
She hasn't learned her lesson yet...
But, today...
I brought my own lunch! ♡
I've got leftovers from last night's supper...
It has Chiaki-sempai's love in it. ♡
WHOOPEE

Huh...?
Chiaki-sempai...?
Wild fantasies... wild fanta-sies...
A fertile mind...
Let's eat. ♡
パカン
FFT
Only locusts
No!!
Thank you for the lunch!
The Death Committee
No....
I can't stand this any-more!!
I'll kill them!!

I'll torture whoever did this!!
ARGHH
Whenever it's something related to food...
Her personality changes...
HALT
スー…
ZZ
ZZ
Z

I caught him...
The culprit!
Him!! (He's the one!?)
Take off that wig!!
Ouch!!
It's my real hair!!
キャーッ
KIYA
It's over so just give up!
No!!
You tricked me!!
Who are you!?
グイッ
TUG
Stop it!!

You're...
Huh...
Masumi-chan, the timpani player!?
Are you guys friends!?
No, but...
We used to be classmates.
We were in the same orchestra...
Let me go!!
Dropout-Taro!
It's Ryutaro!!
Why were you tormenting me!? And what's the Death Committee!?
Everyone's yelling, you're giving me a headache! What's your problem!?
ANGER
ANGER

Anyway, Nodame!
Keep your hands off Chiaki-sama!
Eh...
Oh...
I see...
That explains it.
Huh?
What do you mean? "Explains" what?
What about Chiaki-sempai...?
Chiaki-sama is my Prince...
Though I only watch him from afar... he gives me energy to live and to hope. He's my Apollo!
My source of life.
Apollo-Chiaki

FLPP
Why did I do this!?
Recently, I keep seeing visions of this dirty girl.
Why do you have to be every-where that Chiaki-sama is!?
I can't believe you!!
ギャ～
WOW
Can you make some copies for me?
You live right next to him! Boy, you have a lot of nerve!
Every day you make him cook you dinner!
キィ～
RRRG
Wow, you've done some research...
I can't stand it! You're such a plain Jane!
You're not worthy to grace the same pictures with Chiaki-sama!
Tagaya Saiko looks much better than you!
Plain Jane
ハァ
BREATH
ハァ
BREATH
So what!?
Masumi's not interested in women.
Is some-thing wrong with that?
Ahh...
But... Chiaki-sempai's a man...

I'm challenging you to a battle, Megumi!
You against me!
What?
Yeah, a battle!
Isn't this kind of sudden?
A battle?
I want to prove that I'm a better woman than she is!
She's not gonna get away with this!
A battle of the broads! This should be interesting.
THUMP
THUMP
Well then, how do you want to compete?
On the tympani!
The piano!
How can you do that!?

ALL 3 OF THEM ARE OUT OF THEIR MINDS.
You have to play on an even field!
Like what?
Well for instance...
Let's say 2 weeks from now, on the 24th...
The winner will be the one that gets Chiaki to go out on a date with them!
Agree?
2 weeks from now?
On the 24th?
The Christmas Eve Battle of the Dates!!
Look! Look! Ryu-chan!
Ta-da!
INZAGHI CHRISTMAS
DEC 24th, 2001
DOORS OPEN @ 6:00 PM
STARTS @ 7:00 PM
SECTION: 1 SEAT
¥30.00
It's a "King of Conductors, Inzaghi Christmas Concert Tour" ticket.

Wow, impressive!
キャノ
OOHH
This is a premier ticket, right?
This is special so I went all out! I wonder if Chiaki-sama likes Inzaghi? ♡
Yes! Of course!
He loves orchestras!
He has a soft spot for great performers.
You're spoiling the fun, you're gonna win with this!
HA HA HA
But...
Before I can ask him to go to the concert, I have to be his friend first...
ドキ BEAT
ドキ BEAT
ドキ BEAT
I have to figure out a way to talk to him...
Ohh! But...
What will I do if he says he doesn't want to go out with me!?
I'll just die!! Right there!!
Oh, what am I gonna do? I'm scared!
You'll be fine, just fine! ♡
I'll tell you the secret of how to become Chiaki's friend.

The 24th?
Yes.
Will you go out to eat with me on Christmas Eve?
Huh?
Why do I have to go out with you?
It's for dinner...
We eat together enough.
But I mean... It'd be nice to go out for dinner for a change.
Nnn
!?
Nn Nn
Here, the cellos and violas should play in unison...
Nn Nn
Then clarinets...

IMPRESSED
Sempai...
Pizzicato...
Hn?
Yeah, yeah...
All the trumpets together!
HAPPY
On the 24th I'll clean up my apartment and bake you a cake!!
Yeah...
So would you please come over, Sempai?
All the trumpets together!
むきゃー
SUCCESS WOW
I've already won!
Hey... Look! Look!
This is Hayakawa-kun, isn't it?
Yeah, it is! Wow!
The same one from the conductor's course who went to Germany?
Yeah, yeah!

Must be selected from auditions. Young conductor's gateway to success.
It's pretty amazing that now he's a student at the famous Gerhelm Open Seminar!
HMM?
He looks like the youngest one there, doesn't he?
GULP
Hayakawa is going to attend the Gerhelm lecture!!
Hn...? Oh!
Can I see that?
Sure!
LASSICC JAPAN
Oh...
Chiaki-sama!
Woah
I don't believe it...
Special Press Meeting ~15th Year~ Gerhelm Open Seminar
Open Semina
...Viera-sensei will lecture....
At the seminar...

What's that all about...?

Viera lectures Hayakawa Yukio-kun (22), the only student from Japan.

WHSK
WHSK
WHSK
Nodame, what are you doing?
I'm practicing making a cake.
WHSK
WHSK
No, I mean...
Why are you doing it at school?
Because Christmas is coming soon. ♡
MERINGUE MERINGUE SCOOP
In the end...
Even though I've studied hard on my own... there's nothing I can do with it.

Lesson 8

Even if I write this piece, what good does it do me?
I've already lost to Hayakawa, no matter how hard I've studied.
Just because I can't fly... in the end...
Will I just disappear and remain another unknown in Japan?
Depressed again.
ピーンポーン
DING DONG

Chiaki-sempai!
HEE HEE
Christmas cakes...
Which one would you like?
CHOCOLATE FLAVOR STRAWBERRY
CREAM FLAVOR / TOPPING / JAM
PIZZA FLAVOR / CHEESE / SALAMI / SPONGE
CURRY / MEAT
Christmas?
Why are you asking me that?
Ah... That's when Sempai and I eat will eat cake together for the holy night. ♡
You promised...
GIGGLE
No I didn't!
Uh.....
But... You promised you'd celebrate Christmas Eve with me in my apartment...
I don't care if I promised!
Huh!?
Why would I want to celebrate Christmas Eve with you!?

I'm busy right now!
Don't come over asking me to do useless things!
Leave me alone!!
SLAM
Feed yourself!
SLAM
I.. just...
Who cares about Christmas!
A waste of time!

Being around idiots makes me feel even worse.
Chiaki!
Why...
Ciao!
Chiaki!
Do you have a minute?
Oh, great... Here comes another idiot!
I'm busy!
Go away!
HURRY スタ
HURRY スタ
Eh... Class is over for today, right?
Why don't we go check out the A orchestra rehearsal?
I have a friend that plays timpani.

I don't wanna go!
Mine's friend....
Why not!?
He's really good.
He must be an idiot too.
I'm sure you'll think it was worth it.
No!
He is a genius timpanist with a bright future!
Just take my word for it.
あはは・・
A HA HA
You're kidding me!
Why is he wearing that?
あはは
AHA HA HA
What's the matter with him?
Oh please, Masumi-chan,
this isn't a real concert!

Why are you wearing a tuxedo?
Shut up!
Something wrong with it!?
I stake my life on this rehearsal!
You guys better not make any mistakes!!
GRRR
Eh!?
Why?
It's only a rehearsal.
Because...
Because today....

Chiaki-sama!
You came.... ♡
TK
TK
Foreign teacher
OK...
Today we're gonna begin with the 2nd Movement.
Beethoven's 9th Symphony, 2nd Movement
I hope Chiaki-sama is watching me.
Okuyama Masumi (21)
I'm going to show my deepest feelings for you through my timpani.

Chiaki-sama...
Please, hear all my heart!
げっ
GE
Please
ひく
Huh!?
Be my...

ドドドン
ドーン
DUN DO DUN
オ
Please be my friend! ♡
DISBELIEF
わな
SHOCK
もな…
Stop!
Stop!
Timpani!
GET OUT!!
えっ
Hn!?

Huh...
KLIKLAK
That's your friend?
Mine... ?
Oh... Well ah...
I... uh...
He's the *worst* idiot.

最悪のアホだなー
WORST IDIOT
最悪のアホだなー
WORST IDIOT
…アホだなー
IDIOT
ホールにひびく声
VOICE ECHOING IN HALL
ぶぶ
BRRR
It sounded the best when I listened with my eyes closed.
The orchestra is good, as I expected.

I'm here, but only as an observer...
URAKEN
TING
チーン…
It is with deep regret that I must announce...
To both of you...
NOW SERVING HAMBURG STEAK
VEGETABLE F
RICE / KATS
FRIED RICE
KIM CHI
FRIED RI
SNFF
うっ…
The results of the Christmas Eve Battle of the Dates for Chiaki: You both lost. ♡

わーっ
Why did Sempai all of sudden change his mind!?
He promised me!
WAHH
Why did I get booted from the orchestra!?
I just wanted to express my love to Chiaki-sama!
Was it the wrong idea to make a pizza flavored cake!?
It was the conductor's fault, right!?
It sounds like every-thing went wrong...
Don't come over! Leave me alone!
What am I going to do...
ぶひ
BOO HOO
I have no home and no love to return to now...
You're fine! Look at me...
He's the *worst* idiot.
Instead of becoming his friend, he heaped scorn on me as a human!
You have your own home.

All kidding aside, Masumi-chan, you should have played as usual.
No one's ever seen a dancing timpanist before. That's stupid.
Don't you dance when you play, Mine-kun?
What am I going to do.....
I got kicked out of the orchestra.
Now I have to play all by myself.
I can't stand it!
All alone in a small practice room.
My career is ruined.
My only choice now is to return to Yamagata!!
Don't take it so hard, Masumi...
わーっ
My dream has been shattered and life's gonna be a bitch.
WAH
I envy you guys.
You don't have the kind of pressure I have.
Violin and piano...

Either one of you can play alone...
But I can't shine all by myself...
Masumi-chan....
Hey...
Why can't the 3 of us play in an ensemble?
EH
Piano, violin and... timpani?

Shinichi...
What are you doing for Christmas this year?
You're talking about Christmas too...?
Nothing.
That's what I thought.
I'm having a party at my house again this year. Do you want to come?
Or would you rather you and I spend Christmas together alone?
I wonder if I should bake a cake at your place...
On the 24th I'll clean up my apartment and bake you a cake!!
Ah...
So would you please come over, Sempai?
Yeah... ♫
Now I remember...
Shinichi?
Are you listening?

Saiko... Sorry, I can't.
I'm obligated to see Nodame...
Pizza flavor,
curry flavor...
A promise is a promise, but...
Which flavor...?
I need to refuse...
...politely.
201
NODA
ピンポーン
DING DONG
ピンポン
DING DONG
She's not home.
SILENCE
Never mind.
I'll just tell her next time she comes over.
Hey, you know...
I haven't seen Nodame lately.
For 3 days!

Yeah... me neither.
I usually see her at lunch...
I've heard she's been going to class...
I wonder what she's up to?
She was always sticking around me but...
Has she forgotten about me already?
This world...
It can change so quickly.

Eh... ?
That song... !
Where's your head today? Watch your rhythm!!

I was playing at 120. Why did you change the tempo!?
You messed up the feel!
We were groovin'!
Eh... Was my rhythm off?
Masumi-chan, your rhythm is too stilted.
Hn!
It felt good, but No-DUMMY can't groove!
I don't under-stand...
Like a human metro-nome.
It's NODAME!!
ムキー
GRRR
Take it easy.
Once more from the top.
Why don't we try to loosen it up a little? This is jazz... The feel is what's important.
DRUM SET

That's the song I wrote!
She only heard it one time...
And they made it into a jazz arrangement.

This is a good song. ♡
Of course it's good... Chiaki-sama wrote it. ♡
I'm happy. ♡
Absolutely
But you know...
We need someone to play bass.
It's jazz.
The arrangement doesn't sound natural
Nodame wishes she had another hand.
Then I could play base on the piano!
....

If you need another hand...
I can join you.
What...
UPSET
Your reactions...
Something wrong?
I can't be envious of other people's worlds...

I have to change my world into something good for me.
Whoa!
Wow!
Masumi-chan just fainted!
December 24th
Christmas Eve
SCHOOL
WHSHHH

Nodame, from this point, a little softer, then the violin comes out.
Mine, before your solo, your phrase is clashing.
Disheveled, the fill in measure 36 is 2 beats sooner than you're playing it.
Now play it like I said...
Once more from the top.
What...
Your reactions...
You want to complain?

Give us a break!!
You want to practice until you're satisfied!
You're too picky!!
And don't call me "Disheveled"!!
WAAH
I'm Masumi!
You said we'd have our Christmas party today!!
WAAH
Cake!
Katsudon...!!
Not until you play it perfectly!!
ぎゃぼー
WHAAA!!
Now the ensemble is 4...
URAKEN
And they never got it right before the end of the year because Chiaki was such a perfectionist.

Lesson 9

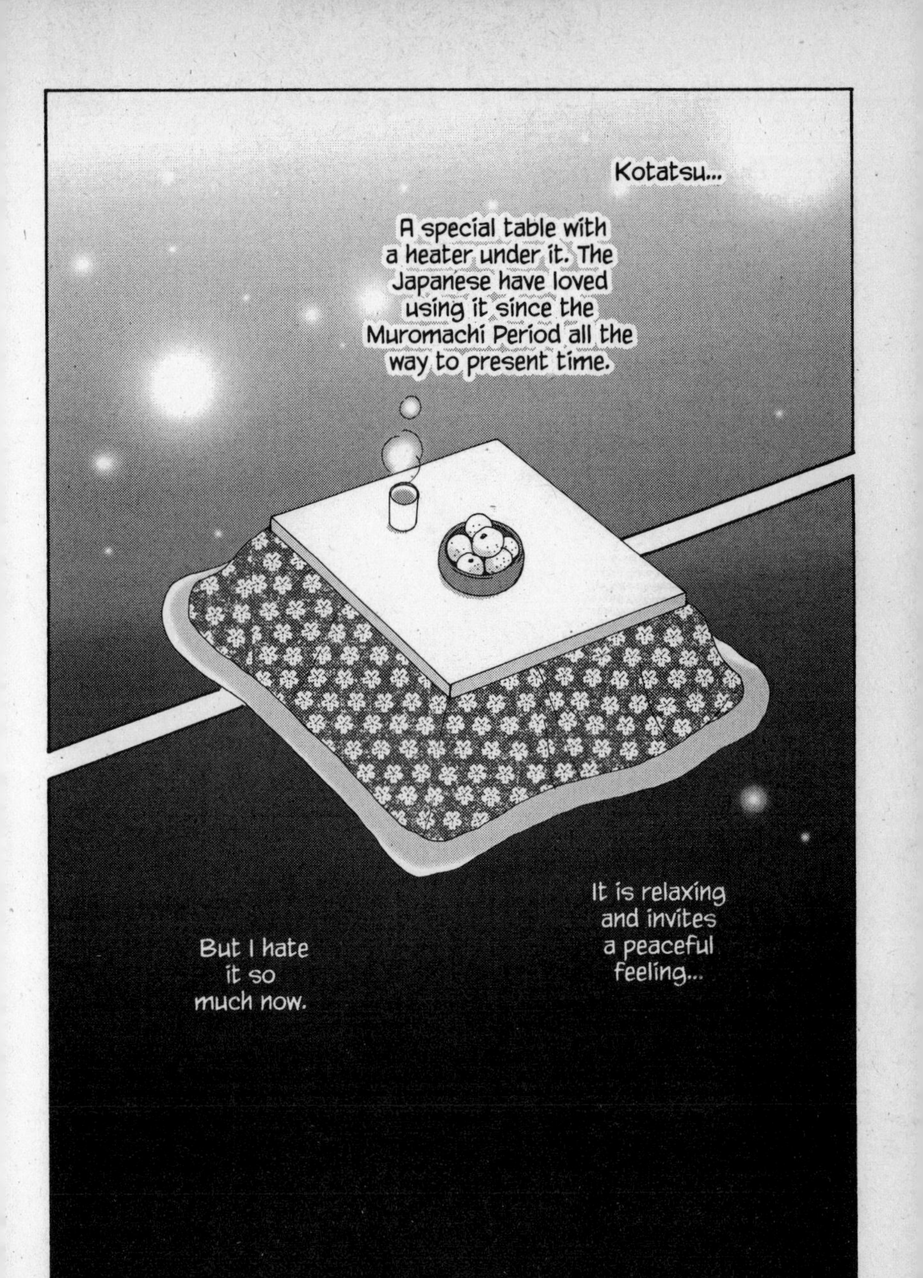
Kotatsu...
A special table with a heater under it. The Japanese have loved using it since the Muromachi Period all the way to present time.
It is relaxing and invites a peaceful feeling...
But I hate it so much now.

It all began at the end of last year...
Hn...? You're not going home to visit your parents?
Nope! Chiaki-sempai isn't going home either, right?
That means I may get my chance. ♡
What kind of "chance"?
A chance for love...
CHUCKLE ♡
Go home!! Go home!!
Go back to the planet you came from!
Don't say that!
Let's make nabe for two. ♡
Nabe!?
My parents just sent me all the ingredients.
PLUNK
VEGETABLES AND MEAT
WEIGHT LOSS TEA

Last time we made nabe it was awful because the locusts tasted so bad. We should try to make a better one. ♡
You made it taste bad...
Hey... These are good mush-rooms.
Dry Seaweed
WEIGHT
What? Some-thing wrong?
Hnn...
Your room is very clean, but I feel like something is missing...
Huh?
I'm trying not to fill it up with a bunch of stuff.
Do you have a problem with that?
Oh...
I know!!

How 'bout this?
Kotatsu!
The only way to eat nabe is with a kotatsu! ♡
PLUNK
What... ?
I don't want that in here!!
EH
You don't?
Of course not!!
I hate that kind of thing.
A table with a futon on it!
You hate it?
There's nothing in the world more comfortable than a kotatsu!
Sempai, you've sat in one before, haven't you?

Actually...
I haven't been in a kotatsu since I was a baby.
EUROPE
When I was young I lived in a foreign country...
In Japan, my mother's parents' house was western style...
There were no tatami rooms in the house.
I had seen kotatsus at friend's houses and on TV a lot...
BUBBLE
BUBBLE
....
UNSURE
ちょん...
Should I put the meat in now?
This is a kotatsu.....
IT'S GETTING... WARM

Warm...
Sempai! The vegetables are ready to eat.
BUBBLE
BUBBLE
ぐつぐつ
Nodame will serve you... because I'm your wife. ♡
だれが妻だ!
Who is!?
Whatever.
INTIMATE ♡
ほのぼの〜
Here, honey.
I'll experience kotatsu this one time...
チュン
CHIRP
チュン
CHIRP
Nnn...

ぷぷ
ZZZZZ
Eh...
...and ended up sleeping in the kotatsu.
Shoot! I ate too much last night....
ZZZZZ
ほが!
I forgot all about practicing piano...
Never mind...
I'll wash the dishes and practice piano after I sleep a little more.
WARM
ぬくぬく〜
WARM
It's hard for me to get out of the kotatsu.

"Hello, Newlyweds!" ♡
WELCOME
It's the end of the year "Love-Love Special!" ♡
WAAA
I envy them. ♡
LOVE LOVE
ラブラブ…
Nodame wants to be on this show. ♡
Ah!
Sempai, good evening.
You have no-shine spiky hair! ♡
YIPEE
キャぴー

LOTS
I went to my room and got some oranges my parents just sent me.
Sempai, do you want some?
Nodame's your wife, so I'll remove the skin for you. ♡
Just a sec...
Why are you wearing your pajamas in my apartment?
Ah, well...
And my TV...
Why is it on the sofa!?
Because you had it sitting on the floor.
The kotatsu was higher than the TV and I couldn't see it.
Then go to your own apartment and watch it!
My room's cold without the kotatsu.
ORANGES

Then take it with you when you leave!
You're not moving into my apartment!!
OK, OK...
I'll go home to my place later...
By the way... would you like a beer?
CAN
Sempai, you slept in the kotatsu so you're thirsty, right?
KIRIN BEER LAGER
GULP
I bought some at the convenience store for you. ♡
You've got a good head on your shoulders.
Oh, the nabe!
I still have a lot of ingredients left.
BUBBLE
BUBBLE
I lost.
KLANG
KLANG
PSH
Let's make it again. ♡
KAA
What-ever...
I'll serve you like I'm your wife. ♡

This year is going to end soon. (no significance)
Sempai, open your mouth. ♡
I'll feed myself!
But... You're my husband!
Uhh....
Hung over....
THROB
THROB
What...
GOWA
ORANG
What's going on!?
My room looks like Nodame's....
N... Nodame!?
Did she leave?
ふう…
WHEW
Finally...
EXHAUSTED

KSHHH
KSHHH
I'll just clean it up later.
WOBBLE
Bath....
I have to wash off Nodame's germs.....
She...
She took a bath in here!?
Nodame...!
SNAP
I'll never let you live here!!

カチャンッ
CLICLICK
LOCK THE DOOR!
I'll return her kotatsu later.
Anyway, I should sleep in my bed again to get back to how it used to be...
ガチャ
KACHA
BEDROOM
ZZ ZZ ZZ Z
Wha...!?
What the hell are you doing!!?

Huhh...
You scared me!
What's wrong, Sempai?
No more nice guy!
What are you doing sleeping in my bed!?
And you took a bath without asking me!!
I'll call the police!
キャ
Get out!
WAH!
But your room and bath are bigger and cleaner than mine!
Nodame hasn't slept in a bed for a long time. That's why!
And you have a bedroom!
You have a bed! It's just under a mountain of garbage!
Go dig it out!!
WAHH!
わ〜ん
I can't!!
ピンポーン
DING DONG
Ah.. Your doorbell!

Who is it?
Express delivery!
Dammit!
ガチャッ
GACHA
Merry end of the year!!
Good evening!
Let's celebrate!!
Uh...
↑ SHOCK
I brought you New Year's Eve fried rice!
HA HA HA
Let's eat and spend New Year's Eve together!!
URAKEN
I brought you sake.... ♡
I heard Chiaki-sama likes sake. ♡
Moon's

Should I call Nodame and have her come over too?
ズカ
PUSH
ズカ
PUSH
I'm coming in... ♡
キャーキャー
EXCITED
This is my first time I'm in Chiaki-sama's apartment. ♡
URAKEN
Huh...?
Mine-kun... Masumi-chan?
Welcome
げっ
EH?
Why are you here?
What were you doing?
Why are you wearing pajamas!?
Nodame's kotatsu...
Nodame's trash...

Chiaki, is she living with you!?
No!!
She's a parasite!!
You have a kotatsu!
HA HA HA
What a great place to have one. ♡
Let's all get in and get warm.
URAKEN
I'll kill you!
Shut up, tatami head!
ギャぼー
GYAAH
I don't know what's going on, but we're all here so we may as well enjoy it!
GRK!
ギギ
URGH
The Battle of the Singers is gonna be on TV soon!
Waoooh! Da Pump! I have to watch it! ♡
ワーー
WOW
Mou Musume, Mou Musume.
"The 9th" will be on soon.....

How did all this happen!?
WA HA HA HA
KYAA! ♡
PIGYAA!
Whoa! What a gaudy dress!
She's lost inside that thing!
She never gets any better, does she? What an awful singer!
Maekawa-sensei hasn't shown up yet?
Who's he?
Maekawa Kiyoshi. ♡
Why do you call him "sensei"!?
Who cares, where's the TV magazine?
WEIGHT LOSS TEA
URAKEN
It's over there.
ORANGES
ORANGES

POING
ひょい
ズズー
KRRRR
TV NEW YEAR
ポコッ
DOINK
MISSED IT
Nodame! Get me sake! More sake!
Well, the snacks are gone.
Nodame! Go buy some more!
ええ~
EH
It's too cold to go out.
You go, Mine-kun.

Not now...
There's a cat sleeping on my foot.
KAKIPOO
GRRR
Where is there a cat!?
A-haa...
You sneaky liar!
Now I understand...
All the bad things that are happening...
...are because of this kotatsu.

This kotatsu has allowed Nodame to impose upon me...

This warm, comfortable futon is very deceptive. It dulls your senses and drains your energy.

If I keep the kotatsu here, it makes it too easy for them to sleep here. And then there's no futon for guests.

Hey!

10,000 yen

Here's some money, go buy some sake and snacks!

バタン
CLOSE
ポーイ
FLOOF
Now that they're gone I can get rid of this stupid thing!
ズルズル
TUG TUG
ガ
CLICK
チャン
CLI
I think now they'll take the kotatsu back to Nodame's.
Maybe the garbage people will go back to the trash can where they belong, too!
ガチャ ガチャ
SHAKE SHAKE
CLI-CLICK
Eh!?
ひ
Ha
WHOOSH

WA HA HA
わはは
Ha! I played it safe and took a key with me!
Ah...
Good thinking!
You're so cruel!
We need the kotatsu!
GRUNT
Put this back in here and we'll have another party!
We'll hear the Joya no Kane soon. ♡
And...
ゴーン
GONG
Happy New Year!
Cheers! ♡

We've had this kotatsu party for 3 days.
THE 9TH
See you!
Bye!
I realized...
My place had turned into a mess... just like Nodame's.
WEIGHT
That's hell on earth.
Hello? I have some bulky garbage I need picked up.

I'm going shopping now. ♡
While the demon isn't here...
BULKY GARBAGE
BULKY GARBAGE
Goodbye, kotatsu.
I'll never sit in you again.

Satisfaction...
はー
AHH...
I'm sorry Nodame, but....
You might change the way you live if the kotatsu is gone...
ピンポーン
DING DONG
Nodame?
Yes?

カチャッ
CLICLICK
Sempai! Sempai! ♡
I just found this really nice kotatsu outside!
BULKY GARBAGE
Now we can each have our own! ♡
わ
WAA
I'm sick of it. I'm begging you!!
Huh?
Chiaki finally realized his enemy wasn't the kotatsu... it was Nodame.

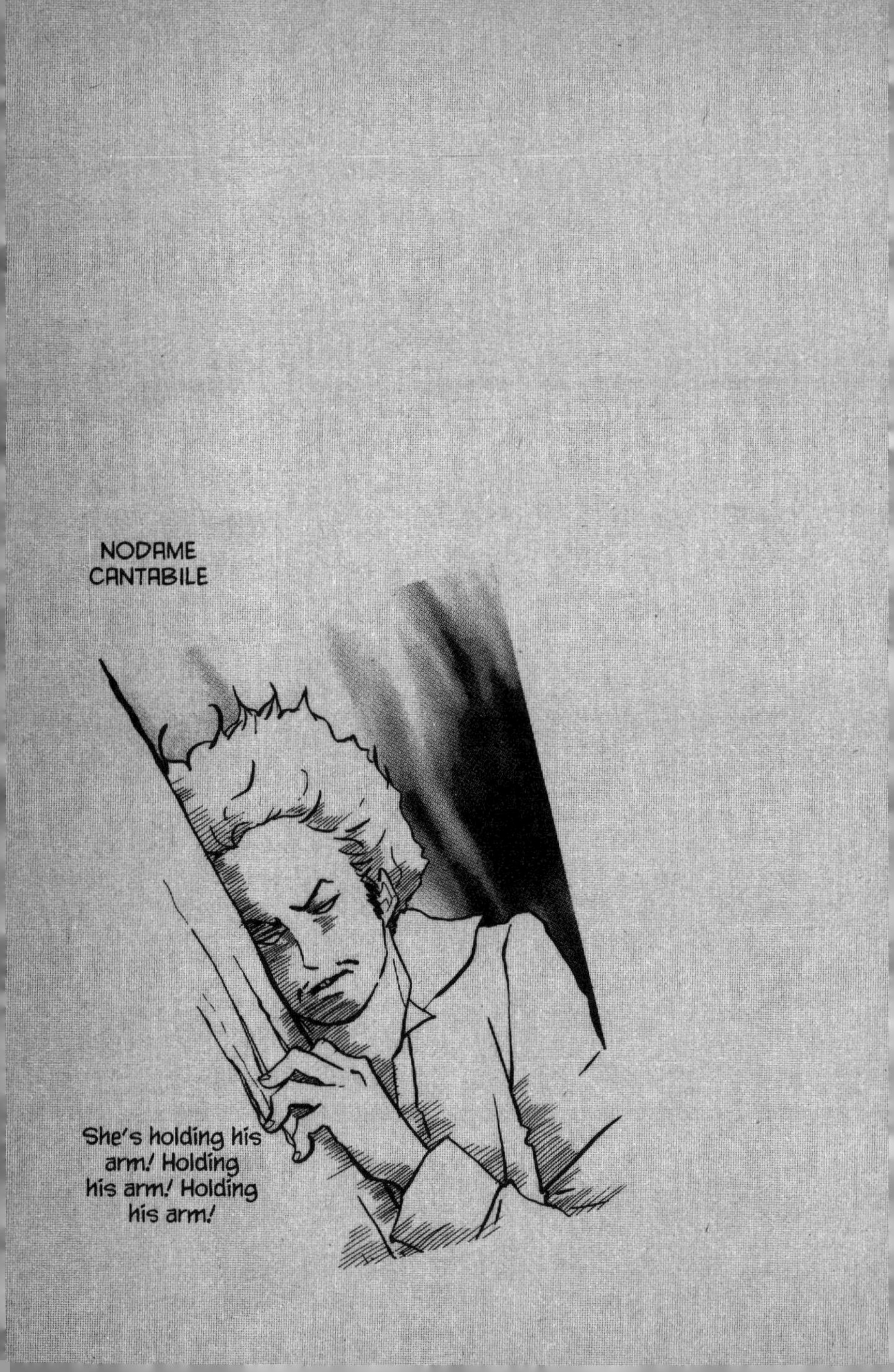
NODAME
CANTABILE
She's holding his
arm! Holding
his arm! Holding
his arm!

Nodame Cantabile
OOPH

Lesson 10

Momongaoka Music Academy
Momongaoka Music Graduate School
Momongaoka Music University
Geisha ♡
Sukiyaki
Roppongi ♡
Sushi

And of course... Geisha...
TOKYO
Who is that foreigner?
Is he a new teacher?
I don't recognize him.
I haven't heard anything about him.

Lately I think...
...my violin playing is much better than before!
PUH!
Who's there!?
WHAM

Hn?
Probably a fan.
DA
DA
DA
FLOOD OF HAPPINESS ♡
YIPEE
I'm happier now than I've ever been!
One month has already passed since I became Chiaki-sama's friend.

A pervert!!
WAOOO
キャー
SNICKER
Did you see that strange old foreign man walking around the school?
Yeah, Yeah!
Think he might be a robber?
Is he a new teacher?
He was watching me in the practice room.
Ew, me too! It's disgusting!

Bravo!
♬
Today's dinner...
...what's it gonna be...?
Excuse me!
Hagya?
Oh... !
You are that...
...fantastic girl!

What a lucky day this is!
Hello...
Can you tell me where I can find a taxi?
Gyabo!?
Foreigner...
Yeah, the taxis are...
Ah!
If you go to a big street, you'll see them everywhere!
Big street... You go that way... Turn left... then right.
CONFUSING
I'm sorry, I can't understand...
ガッ
GRAB
You're very kind.
Please, would you take me there?
Eh...
Then I can take you out to eat. ♡
Eat!?
Sushi... Sukiyaki...
Yes. I'll buy you sushi or sukiyaki... or anything you want.
Well I do feel sorry for him...

But my mom said I shouldn't follow strangers...
Nein... I'm not a bad man.
PASSPORT
I'm Milch Holstein, an honest tourist from Germany.
I have plans to meet my friend tomorrow-row, but I don't have any plans for today.
I'm very lonely. Because I'm an old man...
Alone...
OK!
I'll go out to eat with you. ♡
Oh!
I know a place where the food is really tasty, and it's close! ♡
Let's go there!
Nodame-chan.... ♡
SWEET HOUSE

Oh... ♡
You already cooked a meal!
Then we're just in time! ♡
Today's dinner looks gor-geous...
GOODY
Mmm... it smells good! ♡
Let's eat before it gets cold. ♡
Oh! Here's some wine. ♡
It has a wonderful bouquet.
This is home-made French cooking, no? ♡
HA HA HA
Ah!
Chiaki-sempai... sit down, sit down.
Let's all eat together.
WHANG

Who's house do you think this is!!
You're such a parasite!!
What do you mean... "sit down, sit down"...!?
ほげー
DIZZY
And who's this old man!?
You bring him here without even asking me!
Are you gonna rob me!?
And don't drink my wine!
Nodame-chan... this isn't a restaurant?
It's my boy-friend's apart-ment.
I'm not your boy-friend!!
RRRGH
ボソ
PS
ボソ
PS
Who is this creepy man?!
He isn't a creepy man!
He's my friend!
RIGHT!
I just met him on the street.
His name is... ....
Ah...
You just met!?
Huh..
And you already call him your friend!?

Ah!
Milch!
Milch Holstein! That's his name!
He's German!
That name....
Sounds familiar...
▼German TEXT: Milch
Milch
Holstein
MILK
I'll bet anything that's a fake name!
Oh, Milch...
This is Chiaki-sempai.
He's a sempai at my music college. ♡
Ya! Music college!
Nice to meet you, Chiaki.
No wonder you have a piano.
Yes! Chiaki-sempai is a really good player. ♡

I'd like to hear him play.
Ooh... This is a nice piano.
What is this old man thinking?
Robber?
Chiaki-kun?
Do you know this man?
He is my master for conducting.
Don't grab stuff without asking me!
Conducting...

Is he one of Viera's pupils?
Do you... want to become a conductor?
Something wrong!?
Why are you looking at me like that!?
Nodame-chan...
We should go now.
えっ
EH!
Chiaki-kun looks impatient with us.
Shall we go to the hotel I'm staying at?
But... What about all this food...?
KISS ♡
There is a nice sushi restaurant at my hotel. ♡

Hotel...!?
Come.
Let us go.
Wait...
Wait a minute!
Nodame!
If you want, I'll help you study music after dinner!
Study....
HA HA HA
I can teach you more interesting things than that.
This kind of thing... that kind of thing...
That do you mean, "that" kind of thing?
Maybe the kind of thing Nodame-chan doesn't know.
HA HA HA
This old man.....
You will be all right. Don't be scared.
I've done this hundreds of times.
He's just a dirty old man!

Nodame...
It's OK to sleep here tonight.
In my bed...
With my arm as a pillow.
ぎゃほーっ
YIPEE
Nodame-chan!!

You can see she'd rather stay here.
PURR PURR
With his arm pillow.
SLAM
Glückliche Reise! (Have a nice trip!)
SHINICHI:
Ah...
You can have this.
It was in my mail-box.
FLICK
SLAM
DELIVERY HEALTH
OUT CALL
0X57-587X
SHOCK
わな…
SHOCK
わな

Chiaki...
FUSAAA
Please come in... ♡
Chiaki-sempai. ♡
What are you thinking!
You hopeless idiot! You turd brain!
WAAAH

You're not supposed to bring dirty old men home with you!!
And don't bring all your weird friends here!
Go sleep in your own apartment!!
Liar! Liar!
KYAA
You stole me from him!
THROW
SLAM
Chiaki-sempai's pillow.... ♡
I'll be OK...
Thief...
Idiot... Nodame.

I didn't have time to tell you this.
TRANSFER REQUEST
千秋～っ
Chiaki!
HAA...
Hey, listen!
Big news!

I found out who the new teacher is that's coming to our school!
Listen! Listen! Listen!
He's a super-famous conductor! It's Stresemann!
Hn...?
Stresemann...?
Franz Von Stresemann...
He's a German master... Vienna... Berlin... London... He's conducted great orchestras all over the world!

I don't believe it...
Why would such a famous conductor come to a college in Japan?
HA HA HA
I'm not kid-ding!
I heard he's known the school's director for many years.
Oh man!
If you don't believe me, go see for yourself.
He's in the teacher's room right now.
No way...
That's too good to be true. Right when I decided to transfer to the conductor's course.

HA
HA
HA
Your Japanese is very good... especially your compliments.
All women teachers are beautiful.
M-hmm.
IMPRESSIVE
I don't believe it...
You see!?
Stresemann is really here!?
He's the real thing, but he looks different from how I imagined.

You'd like to start a new student orchestra?
Huh?
He looks totally different from his photos!!
That dirty old man...
...is Stresemann!?
With students I choose.
Yes.
My personal orchestra.
Younger
Yes, of course I do.
The new orchestra is more for fun.
We had hoped that you would want to instruct our A orchestra and the conducting class.
NERVOUS
B... But....

I'd like to give my lessons to as many students as possible and give them all the chance to perform.
For the year I'm in Japan, I'd like to accomplish as much as possible.
Sensei....
What a great master you are....
In fact, I've already chosen my students for the orchestra.
SCATTER
Please notify the students in these photos.

Bought them in Shibuya

Are you sure about this?
Timpani
Concert master
?
What's the matter, Chiaki?
What if my transfer is denied...

Lesson 11

"Stresemann Special Orchestra"
STRESEMANN SPECIAL ORCHESTRA
No way...
Is this serious? Stresemann!?
ザワ
ザワ
MUMBLE MUMBLE
Hey look! I was chosen!
Huh... Me too!
Shoot!
What standards were they judged on?
Who chose these members?
Violin
MINE RYUTARO
Timpani
OKUYAMA MASUMI

MASCOT GIRL
NODA MEGUM
Stresemann! I'm gonna play in Stresemann's orchestra!
YEAH
I made it!
Great!
WOW
003
05:32
I still remember when I heard Mahler's 8th with Stresemann conducting...
I couldn't imagine anyone conducting Mahler's music so beautifully.
And now...
...I was shocked.
I find out he's a pervert.
Shocked

There's no chance for me to have lessons from the great master any more.
I want to study in foreign countries, but I can't.
Even so... I still want to learn from him!
I've got to transfer to the conducting course!!
Milch!
Why wasn't I chosen to play piano in your orchestra!?
Because you're the orchestra's "mascot girl."
HA HA HA
You just have to stay by me.
MONTHLY EROTIC
Why? What's that for?
Just for me. ♡
HA HA HA
But my piano....
What!? You want to transfer, Chiaki-kun?

Chiaki?
Yes.
To the conductor's course...
Chiaki-sempai's gonna transfer!?
↑ EARS LIKE A BAT
I've been thinking about it for a long time, but...
I've finally decided...
Here...
TRANSFER REQUEST
I'm going to submit it today.
I see.
Conducting...
Your piano...
I was interested in how it was progressing.

Sensei...
Thank you for...
No! Sempai!
Don't transfer!
Here she is again.
If you transfer...
We won't be able to play piano together any more!
We always play together at my place!
But if you change courses, I'll never get to see you!
SNAG
Calm down, Noda-kun....
No!
Don't quit piano class!
What are you talking about!?
RIP RIP

I won't allow you to transfer to the conducting course.
FLUTTA FLUTTA
パタ パタ
Because I despise you.
You make me ill.
But....
Milch
Why?
I may be a great master, but I'm also just one of the teachers.
TRANSFER
You don't have the right to do this!
That can't be your reason!!
These things happen often...
Immature!
...in this world.

I'm also a human before I'm a teacher...
And *I'm* capable of making mistakes too.
So I don't have the right, but I do have the power.
If I say it's blue, it's blue... even if it's red.
What is he talking about...?
Old man...
Are you jealous of me because I stole Nodame from you!?
That was...
FH
...of little conse-quence.
You told me that you're a pupil of Viera's?
Huh...
It was 15 years ago that I met Viera for the first time...
I still remember it.

It was at a small toy store in London.
I've looked in 3 stores and I finally found it.
I've looked in 5 stores.
I want to give it to my grand-child!
My grandchild, Chelsea!
You aren't married!!
Who's Chelsea?

Well...?
There was a party the day before yesterday where you tried to talk a married woman into going out with you. That was my wife.
You're very rude. Don't you know who I am!?
Yeah, I know you well.
I've heard rumors that you sexually harass and have affairs with women from your orchestras...
I've heard a lot about you.
!!
Thank you, come again!
I couldn't believe that such a jerk could have such a beautiful wife.
He made me very angry!
Hey
Wait a minute!
You still hold a grudge because of a toy!?
A woman!

So you can just reject a student who wants to learn from you because of a stupid reason like that!?
Of course!
Your master is my enemy... and that means you're my enemy too!
I have to nip this in the bud before it grows.
If you want to blame someone, blame your master.
CLOP
カツ
カツ
CLOP
Devil
Sempai... Maybe you should give up trying to transfer to the conducting course. ♡
Small devil

CHATTER
ザワ
ザワ
CHATTER
PANT
はぁ
PANT
はぁ
I made it!
I was in a hurry to get here, even though I don't have class today.
Me too...
AH HA HA
WOW
I'm so excited to be chosen for Stresemann's Special Orchestra!
It's still early to be here.
We're meeting without our musical instruments today, right?
I wonder why?
Ah... I'm nervous.
Here he comes!
Hi every-body!

I realize this was on short notice.
Thank you all for coming today. ♡
おお〜っ
OHHH
IT'S REALLY STRESE-MANN!
He speaks Japan-ese well.
I personally chose each one of you to be members of my Special Orchestra.
From today, we are going to be like family.
But to be a real family takes time and we have to try hard.
A "Roman orchestra wasn't built in a day."
Wow, clever!
That's beautiful, great master...
He's a god...
I'd like to get to know all of you as soon as possible...
And so...
Today, we are going to have an aikon.

WHAT!?
They are very popular in Japanese culture. An aikon will give us the chance to get to know each other.
I researched it. ♡
At the aikon we can talk about music...
...and everyone can have a good time!
KABUKICHOU
UTSUBOHACHI
うつぼ八
HA HA HA
Heh!
I don't think he under-stands what an aikon is for.
Aikon...
Yeah...
Let's go. ♡
HA HA HA

CLAP
CLAP
CLAP
Drink! Down it!
A boy-friend...!?
CLAP CLAP CLAP
GLUG GLUG
Do you have one?
GASP
No, I don't.
Really? You don't have one? ♡
DRUNK
HA HA HA
Amazing....
He seems to know exactly what aikons are for!
Chug it down!
HA HA HA
Flute girl... What's your name?
AH...
I'm Suzuki.

Viola girl... What's your name?
Your first name...
I'm... Mika.
Ah..
And what do you play?
Hey! Dancing girl!
Can you please dance for me?
Dancing girl!?
WA HA HA
This is fun!
THE NUT-CRACKER
Hey...
Is that really Stresemann?
Huh?
His name is Milch Holstein-san, isn't it?

Do you think he's a fake?
PSSS
PSSS
Yeah....
He speaks very good Japanese.
KYA HA HA
He sure acts undignified.
And he's nasty!
Hey, Nodame.
HA HA HA
HEE
Is it true Chiaki said he wanted to transfer to the conducting course?
Yeah...
Ahh...
But Milch tore his request into little pieces. ♡
He tore it up!?
That's too bad.
If Chiaki had transferred to the conducting course his graduation would have been pushed back.
Huh?
I don't think he could graduate from the conducting course in only a year.
He may have gone to a graduate school or . . .
Who knows.
Ah....!?

I wonder if Chiaki plans to go to Europe after he graduates?
It won't be any fun here without him.
"what's-his-name," the Great Master...
Europe...
Milch!
Chiaki-sempai's transfer request...
Oh... mascot girl...
Hmm...
I want you to approve it!
PATA
TRANSFER REQUEST
PLEASE TRANSFER ME TO THE CONDUCTING COURSE! CHIAKI SHINICHI
COMMITTING CRIME

The yellow handker-chief of happiness. ♡
Eh... Chiaki..
TRANSFER
FLOOOG
びーむ
TOSS
ポーイ
Calm down, Nodame-chan.
Come sit on my knee and have a drink! ♡
SHOCKED
ドヤーン
Rrrgh!
Chiaki-sempai!

WITHDRAWAL NOTICE
What..
What is that!?
You're quitting!?
Hey... This is a library...
WITHDRAWAL NOTICE
Well... I think I should go to a better college...
One without weirdoes
HNNK
Ah...
TOSS
Let's go directly to the president...
...and ask him about your transfer!
Come on!!
↖ DESPERATE
Ah!
TUG
Nodame!?
PRESIDENT'S OFFICE

BAM
Mr. President!!
What can I do for you, Nodame-chan?
You!?
The president went to buy me some cigarettes.
Would you like me to give him a message for you?
Nodame... It's no use....
The president's on his side...
Let's go...
Milch!!
You're my friend, aren't you!?
PETITION WITH TEARS
Please grant me my wish!!

Nodame-chan...
I see...
I admit defeat.
Very well then... If you'll kiss me, I'll grant you Chiaki's transfer. ♡
GULP
Then you haven't completely lost yet!
I almost have.
You know, kissing is no big deal in America. ♡
He does have a point.
He grew up in Europe.
You're actually considering this!?
SERIOUS
Well, it's a big deal for me!
Kiss... he transfers...
No kiss... no transfer. ♡
Gold hatchet...
...or silver hatchet?

I wonder if Chiaki plans to go to Europe when he graduates?
Europe...
Or kiss.....
PTT
EH...
え
Nodame?
He's late.
Old man!

▲ Everybody thinks that they're the only good player.

はあ
PANT
はあ
PANT
はあ
PANT
So....
Now what are you going to do?
I wasn't expecting for you to hit him.
I thought she was gonna kiss him.
POTATO CHIPS
But... all of a sudden he grabbed me and...
Is he dead?
.....♡
He looks like he's dreaming!
About women!
Then just leave him here. He'll wake up.
Shouldn't we...

Ah....
Oh I forgot!
There's a rehearsal today.
I'm not gonna wait any longer.
I'm sorry, but I'm leaving!
Chiaki-sempai.
Can you conduct?
Huh?

I WAS COLD SO I PUT ON MY HAT.

Milch isn't feeling good...
So today, this person's going to conduct!
Oh...
Huh!?
お
CHIAKI!?
千秋ー!?
キャー
WOW
キャ
WOW

NODAME CANTABILE

Lesson 12

BEETHOVEN

NUTCRACKER
NODAME CANTABILE

I'm going to conduct this orchestra!?
Chiaki-sama's gonna conduct!?
キャー
WOW
Why is Chiaki conducting?
ザワ
RUSTLE
ザワ
RUSTLE
キャ
WOW
Isn't he in the piano course?
Chiaki, are you going to be able to conduct?
He's good enough!
How do you know!
ぷぎゃっ
WHACK

What...
What song?
Ah...
Beethoven's 7th Symphony!
Milch's score.
Chiaki's going to conduct... This is going to be fun.
The 7th...
I recently listened to Viera's CD of this piece, and it had inspired me to study it.
Yeah!
I can do this!!
Every-one...
Did you practice?
We'd already decided to learn this one at the aikon the other day.
I practiced at home. ♡
Me too, it's per-fect!
Well, let's get rehearsing with Chiaki before the old man shows up!!

*The first violin player and leader of the orchestra

I don't feel good about this, but...
Why don't we start from the first movement?
Ah!
Shoot...
No baton....
I have one from one of my other classes... you can use it if you want. ♡
No! Please use mine!
It's a little more expensive.
SHOVE
Mine's brand new, I just bought it!
I could conduct without one.
L!H-UHH!
Then let's do paper-rock-scissors!
I don't understand why Shinichi Chiaki is so popular and charismatic at this college...
HN...
So he's a good piano player and he looks cool... I doubt he can conduct.
HMM
I'm better looking than he is...

I bet he'll just pretend to conduct.
Hmm... I guess we'll see.
I'll show Chiaki-sama how good I am.
No dancing this time.
I'll show them all that I'm a great Concert Master!!
TP
OK...
Even though I'm just filling in for orchestra rehearsal, I know I can conduct.
I can't pass up this chance.
Let's begin.
This is exciting!

URGHH
TUG
TUG
URGHH
Milch! Wake up!
I want you to see Chiaki-sempai conduct!
I've never seen it either, but I bet he'll do good job.
He's great at everything he does.
I'm sure you're going to like him!
Hey...!
WHACK
SLAP
GRAB

Beethoven's 7th Symphony in A Major.
DUNNN
This composition is the most pleasing and comprehensible symphony in his repertoire.
The introduction begins with a powerful A Major chord.
And then the melody is played by the oboe.

Stringed instruments play a full major scale
Wha...?
Eh...
Huh...
GNNN
ポ
SQUEEK
キコ
キコ
SQUEEK
ぷオー
HNN
Watch it!!

What kind of orchestra is this!?
They're awful!!
Sounds horrible!
I know it's only the first rehearsal...
But how can they make Beethoven sound so bad!?
Maybe the old man only chose the awful players and weirdoes from the school!?
Hnn...
THROB

They finished playing it for the first time.
Phew
Hey, everybody! The 7th sounded cute, but...
Shouldn't we play it more grandiose?
Louder and heavier!
What do you mean, "grandi-ose"!?
FWIP
OUCH
いでっ
Don't even suggest that at your level!!
Eh?
You made mistakes all over the place!
The Concert Master shouldn't be screwing up the orches-tra!!
UHHH
Did you really practice!?
SNICKER
The Concert Master looks mis-erable.
Your pitch is bad!
Are you really a music student?
HN
SHOCK
Horn 2!
Don't break for a breath on the fortissimo! You disap-point me!

Second clarinet! Your sound is awful!
Don't make that peep peep sound!
Viola!
You!
Your sound is harsh! Also play more "piano."
I have a lot to tell each person, but it just goes on forever!
We'll try it again from the beginning in 5 minutes.
MURMUR
Chiaki is scary.
Strict
Suffering...
MURMUR
Chiaki-sama is great! ♡
He's just like a real conductor.
His baton waving is beautiful. ♡
AHHH
Yeah?~ ♡
You imagine too much.
"Don't make that peep peep sound!"
UPSET
How dare he insult me in front of Kaoru-san...
My reed just wasn't working right.

How dare he act like that!
Right!
After all, he's only playing as a conductor.
He just talks big.
Hn
Should we make fun of him?
Hey....
SNICKER
He just pointed out the easy mistakes that everyone noticed.
Ready!
Let's begin!
I have the chance to conduct an orches-tra...
And Beethoven composed this wonderful song...
I'm going to make it work!
It doesn't matter how I feel about their technique, I don't have a choice.

ジャーン
JUNNN
Violin...
Play your 16th notes a little softer and more clearly!
Horn 2, fortissimo!
You're behind!
Cello girl!
AH... は
You're flat, play it a little higher. And play your parts more clearly.
Wow... Chiaki-sempai's ear is really good...
He can pick out every sound.
Huh, Milch?

Milch?
Stop! Sto-o-op!!
やり直しっ
Once more.
Horn 2! You came in early this time!
Second clarinet!
You're falling behind!
もう～
Jeez...
下手…
You're awful.
Maybe there are some people in this orchestra that can't play.
Hmm?
Yeah, like you!!
This orchestra is disgusting....
Everything is awful.
The rhythm is so bad.
I feel sorry for Chiaki-sama.
It's not pa pa pa pah. It's pahn!
Play a little more "piano" after that...
OK. Once more from there...

When it will be difficult for him to hear it, we're gonna switch the oboe and clarinet parts.
GLANCE
チラ
Heh... Chiaki, watch what I'm gonna do...
Chiaki won't be good enough to notice.
Cl.
Dolce
And when rehearsal is over...
A HA HA
I kind of screwed up and played the wrong part.
Me too...
HUH
I'm glad that Chiaki didn't notice anything wrong. ♡
HA HA HA
I'm gonna put him to shame!!
↖ GETTING REVENGE
Now!!

RRRG
EH...
He notices!
UHH...
UH-OH
FRUSTRATED
Cellos again!
Pay attention!
Watch your pitch!
Horn 2! You're late again!
Viola!
Too loud! How many times do I have to tell you!?

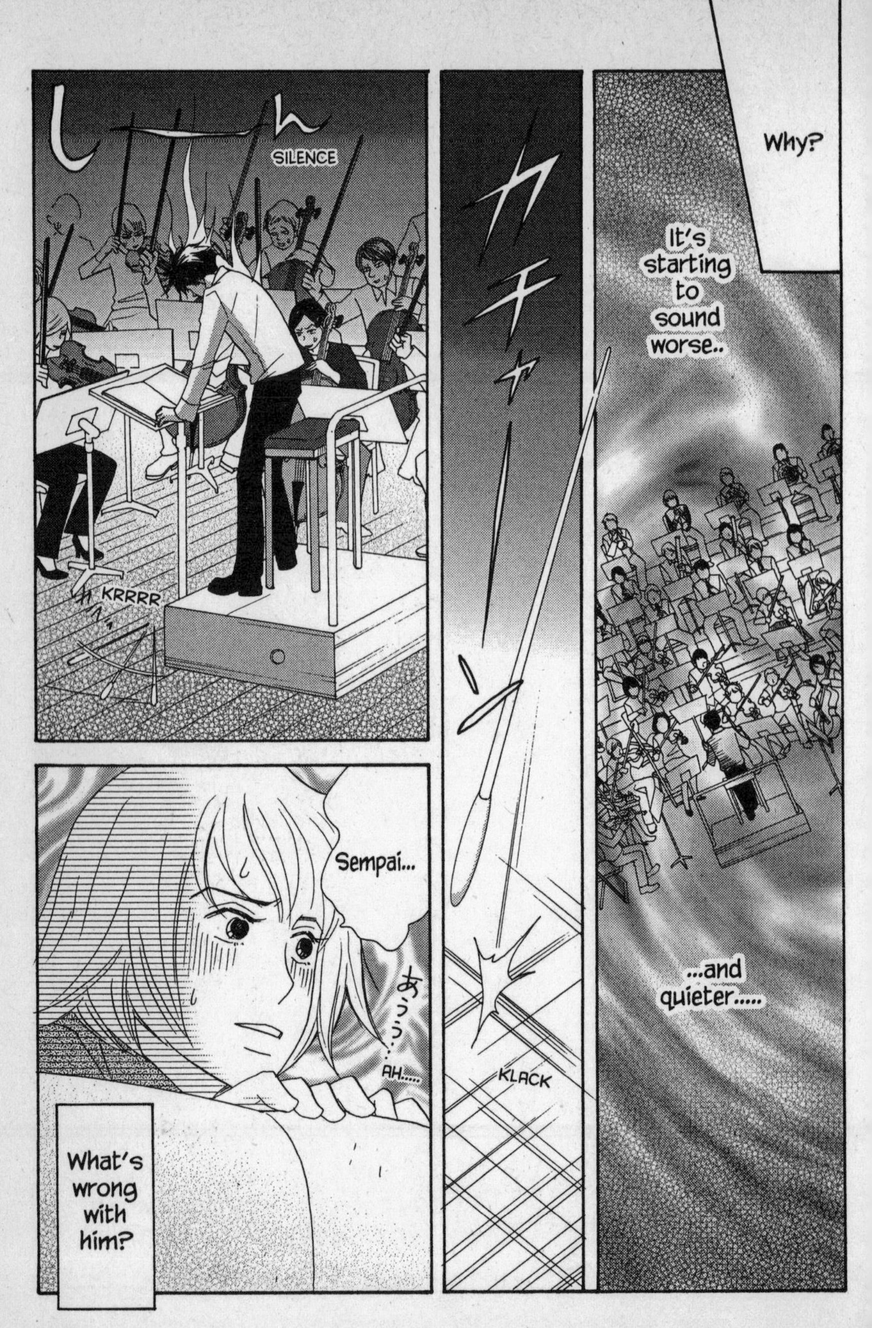
Why?
It's starting to sound worse..
...and quieter.....
カチャーン
KLACK
しーーん
SILENCE
KRRRR
Sempai...
あうう...
AH.....
What's wrong with him?

There are some players trying to give me a hard time.
They don't have the ability to learn.
They ignore my directions.
I'm sick of conducting such an unpleasant orchestra!!
CLAP
CLAP
OK! That's enough!
CLAP
Chiaki, You have failed...

Milch!
Thank you for waiting, everybody! It's time for the real conductor to play his role!
おおーーっ
OHHH
OLD MAN
GREAT MASTER
Huh, I failed...?
Why!?
You made that girl cry.
That's the worst type of failure you could be!
VEXING!
SNIFFLE
Don't cry, Shizuka-chan....
YOUR FACE IS BIG.
That's a girl!?
The viola player...
A different shock.
And that's why?

Now
WHA...
Gather yourselves and let's play once more from the beginning!
Oh... Mine-kun...
EH...
First of all, don't worry about your bowing technique.
Just make it sound happy.
Like you always do.
Ah... OK!
Horn boy...
If you don't feel good, take it easy today.
Y....
ズピ…
SIGH
Yes sir!
Clarinet boy...
It sounds like you may need to change your reed.
Disgusting
Yes!!
IMPRESSED

Bowing is how to use the bow on a stringed instrument.

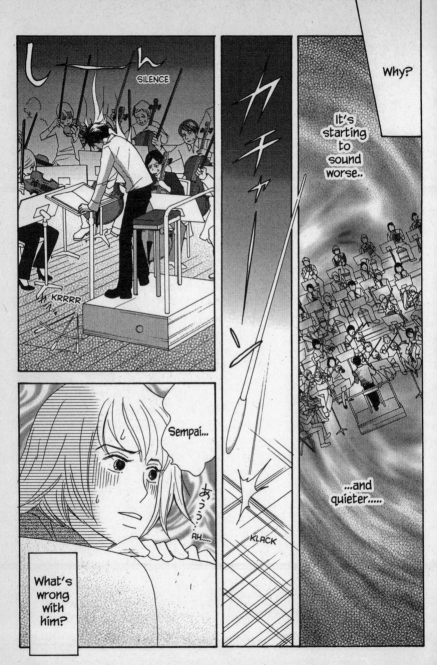

Miho-chan on the cello...
It's all right for you to be fascinated by me. ♡
EH
But, then please make your cello sound sexy. ♡
OK!
And crybaby on the viola....
I didn't know what happened to you...
But you can only be wild at parties. Please....
WAHOO!
どっ
DOH
あははは
A HA HA
At the aikon the other day...
Shizuka-chan was so wild!
OK, as Chiaki said...
Let's play though it once more.

Reeds and your well-being are one's own responsibility.
Awful is awful.

But...
When he conducts, the orchestra starts to sing.
"as Chiaki said"? This is...
...the same?
No....
That man respects...

Music...
and people...
So he gets respect back from them.
I have a long way to go...

He is a real Great Master.
TRANSFER REQUEST
PHEW
RIP
RIP
RIP
You can tear it up as many times as you want.
FWIP
TRANSFER REQUEST
I'm going to keep giving them to you until you accept me as your pupil.

You don't have to transfer to get to be one of my pupils.
Eh?
Actually, I am interested in teaching you, but...
I think you're wasting your talents by being Viera's pupil.
And you shouldn't transfer.
You should continue in the piano course.
But then...
When you're not studying piano you should always be at my side.
Sensei...
But that means...

OK! Enough of that. Let's go to Shibuya to celebrate!
HUH?
AHHH...
If I'm with Chiaki....
The girls will all come running!
CRASH
NOOOO!
Milch, you're an idiot!!
What kind of pupil do you want Chiaki-sempai to be!?
For girls!?
What!!
I'm not gonna let you have Chiaki-sempai!!
はぁ....
HAAA
We are two people as one!
Please return to Germany

Then now that I have Chiaki, I get a free Nodame as well!
SQUEEZE
No!
HEEEEE
STOP IT!
Who could imagine that my debut as a conductor would end in failure...
Hey, let's go home..
M-hm
But end up turning my life around and changing my destiny.
Again...

–Me and music–

I was an elementary school student
I got a big shock the first time I recorded myself and heard my singing.
I was tone deaf. I still am.

Thank you for helping me in my research!
Nodame, Makiron
Hoshino-kun,
Okuyama Takushi-kun

Best wishes to everybody!

Nodame
Cantabile

Translation Notes

Japanese is a tricky language for most Westerners, and translation is often more art than science. For your edification and reading pleasure, here are notes on some of the places where we could have gone in a different direction in our translation of the work, or where a Japanese cultural reference is used.

Masumi, page 8

Masumi is a gay male in love with Shinichi. In this scene, he is referred to as a "she."

Nabe, page 13

A department store in Japan can be compared to a mall in America. Different shops can lease space in the same building. Some department stores have a food section with vendors selling bread, lunches, candy, etc. A department store with a large food section is a joy to find because the shops usually offer many samples to try.

Locusts—not just for killing crops, page 16

Not for everyone, but locusts have long been considered a delicacy in Japan . . . just takes a little teriyaki sauce to bring out the flavor. Zasai is a pickled Korean dish, much more popular than locusts (and probably tastier)!

LOCUSTS
ZASAI
SPRING ROLLS
These were the only things I could read...

Dry tangle, nappa, and shungiku, page 17

Dry tangle is a type of dried seaweed used in soups, nappa is a cabbage that is very popular in Asian stir-fries, and shungiku is edible chrysanthemum leaves. These are all common ingredients for soup, especially in nabe.

Dropout-Taro, page 22

Mine's last name is Ryutaro, so "Dropout-Taro" is a play on his name.

Katsudon, page 60

Katsudon is a dish made from chunks of pork deep-fried in a soup with soy sauce and sugar. It is served on a bed of white rice and it is very popular in Japan.

The Muromachi Period, page 62

The Muromachi Period was the era in historical Japan from 1338 to 1573 when Ashikaga Takauji appointed himself shogun and established his government in Kyoto. Named after the district where the government buildings were located, it was a time of much fighting for control of Japan.

The tatami room, page 66

A tatami room is simply a room with tatami mats for the floor. Tatami mats are durable rectangular mats made from tightly woven straw. In Japan, they are used for everything from sitting to walking on, and are comfortable enough to even sleep on.

In Japan, my mother's parents' house was western style...
There were no tatami rooms in the house.

The Battle of the Singers, page 78

Every New Year's Eve in Japan, there is a TV show that has a "Battle of the Singers," males vs. females. Families throughout Japan gather around their TV sets to watch the contestants embarrass themselves.

Mou Musume and Da Pump, page 78

Mou Musume is a shortening of the name Morning Musume, which is a vocal group in Japan. Da Pump is also a vocal group currently popular in Japan.

Maekawa Kiyoshi, page 79

Maekawa Kiyoshi is a popular singer in Japan who appeals mostly to an older crowd and is known for singing traditional Japanese music.

The Joya no Kane, page 84

The Joya no Kane is a big bell that is rung 108 times on New Year's Eve. It is believed that this yearly ritual helps you start the New Year with a healthy body and spirit.

Geisha, page 92

Geisha are a class of professional women in Japan who have devoted themselves to entertaining men. "Geisha" literally translates to "arts person," which is exactly what a geisha is: a woman trained in the traditional arts of Japan. They entertain with traditional dance, song, and music.

Sukiyaki, page 92

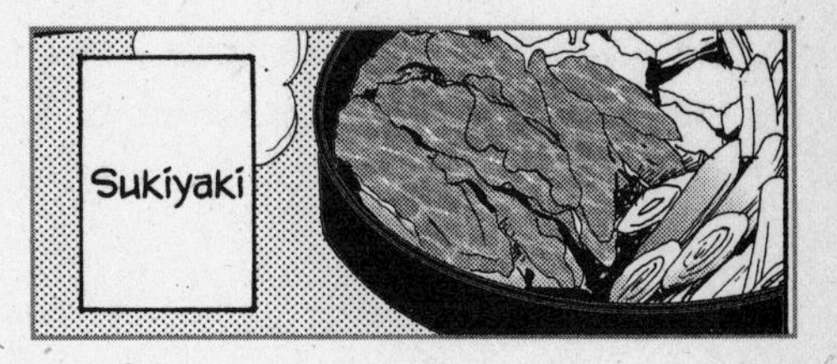

Sukiyaki is thinly sliced beef and vegetables cooked in a pot with soy sauce, sake, and sugar. It's usually made in a pan right on the table and is great for friendly gatherings.

Roppongi, page 92

Roppongi is an area in Tokyo known for its nightlife, where the highest concentration of foreigners can be found. Roppongi is also known for its cosmopolitan feel, stylish clothing stores, and high-class restaurants.

Sushi, page 92

Sushi is a popular food in Japan most commonly made of slices of fish atop balls of rice. Other common ingredients are raw vegetables and

seaweed. Sushi may have gotten its start in Japan, but sushi bars can now be found around the world as a testament to how tasty it is.

Nein!, page 100

"Nein" means "no" in German.

The aikon, page 131

An aikon is a social gathering where friends bring more friends for the purpose of meeting potential dating partners. When the students hear Franz announce that they are going to have an aikon, they are naturally mystified and joke that he doesn't understand the purpose of one. But once at the club, it becomes apparent that he knows exactly what it is for, as he parties and flirts with all the girls.

"Piano," page 161

"Piano" in musical direction means "play softly."

Nodame-speak

Nodame is...different. She often uses a nonsense language that includes words like "Gyabo!" and "Muki." Nodame-speak doesn't make sense, but you can get the gist of Nodame's feelings from the context.

Preview of Volume 3

We're pleased to present a preview from Volume 3. This volume will be available in English on November 29, 2005, but for now you'll have to make do with Japanese!

行ってきま――す！
ありがとう
親友――！
愛してマース♡
裏軒
はーー
脱力…
オレの
実技試験は
10時からだから
……
家に帰るほど
時間はないな
……疲れた
あいつら
進級したら
3年か――……

ガラッ
いらっしゃ——い!!
レバニラハンバーグランチ!
はいよ!!
レバ・ハンランチー!
え?
ランチ!?
ええぇ——!?
11:30
おや先生
お目覚めですか?

お目覚めって……
なんで起こしてくれなかったんですか――!?
毛布
え……?
まくら
だって疲れてるだろーし起こしちゃ悪いと思って……
あれ？先生
もしかしてなんか用事あったの？

いいじゃ――ん！ちゃんと追試受ければ
千秋は留年なんかしねーよ！
今度はのだめがちゃんと起こしてあげますから♡
のだめの恩返しデス！
追試になると評価は60％……
どんなにがんばっても「S」はつかなくなるんだよ
オレは「A」なんてとったことないんだ――!!
おまえらのせいだー
わー
一生の汚点だー
ムカー
人のことよりまず自分……と千秋は学習したのだった

はぁ
ガラ
ガラ
ガラ
はぁ……
あと少し……
はー
はー
あと少しで学校!!

ねぇねぇ！
ちょっとなにあれ～～～!?
楽器が歩ってる!!
妖怪・コントラバス!?
あはは
人間みえないじゃ～ん
ちょっと……
マキちゃんマキちゃん
ぶ！本当だ～～っ
マキちゃんのお弁当も歩ってるよ……
のだめ――!!
ひー
あざやか…
妖怪・弁当ドロボー

ドンッ!
どべしゃーん
ぎゃぼ——!!
もが〜〜っ
「モーソン」の"春の行楽弁当"が〜〜!!
あ……あのっ!
そのお弁当……いらなかったら
わたし食べてもいいですか?

はう?
でも……
中身が落ちて
砂が……
大丈夫
です!
空腹は
最高のスパイス
ですから!
ガツ ガツ
ガツ ガツ
ガツ ガツ
ふおお~~~
しゅごい……
スパイスって……砂!?
はっ
いけない!
オケの練習
遅刻してるん
だった!!
つい食べものに
目がくらんで……
のだめちゃん
ごちそーさま
――!
カタカタカタカタ

GENSHIKEN

The Society for the Study of Modern Visual Culture

VOLUME 2

BY KIO SHIMOKU

SAVE THE GENSHIKEN!

Kanji Sasahara has finally accepted that he's a true otaku who belongs in the Genshiken. Meanwhile, Saki Kasukabe still can't stand how much time her boyfriend, video game master Kousaka, wastes with the Genshiken guys.

Saki isn't the only one who's upset that the club members do nothing but sit around playing video games. Kitagawa, the vicious vice president of the campus activities organization, is determined to break up the Genshiken. What's an otaku club to do?

Ages: 16+

Includes special extras after the story!

VOLUME 2: On sale July 26, 2005

For more information and to sign up for Del Rey's manga e-newsletter, visit www.delreymanga.com

VOLUME 1
BY SATOMI IKEZAWA

Ages 13+

Ponta is a normal Labrador retriever puppy, the Koizumi family's pet. Full of energy, she is always up to some kind of trouble. However, when Grandpa Koizumi, a passionate amateur inventor, creates the "Guru Guru Bone," which empowers animals with human speech, Ponta turns into a human girl!

Surprised but undaunted, Ponta ventures out of the house and meets Mirai Iwaki, the most popular boy at school. Saved by Mirai from a speeding car, Ponta reverts to her normal puppy self. Yet much has changed for Ponta during her short adventure as a human. Her heart throbs and her face flushes when she thinks of Mirai now. She is in love! Using the power of the "Guru Guru Bone," Ponta switches back and forth from dog to human, but can she win Mirai's love?

WINNER OF THE KODANSHA MANGA OF THE YEAR AWARD!

Includes special extras after the story!

VOLUME 1: On sale July 26, 2005

For more information and to sign up for Del Rey's manga e-newsletter, visit www.delreymanga.com

TOMARE!

[STOP!]

You are going the wrong way!

Manga is a completely different type of reading experience.

To start at the *beginning*, go to the *end!*

That's right! Authentic manga is read the traditional Japanese way—from right to left. Exactly the *opposite* of how American books are read. It's easy to follow: Just go to the other end of the book, and read each page—and each panel—from right side to left side, starting at the top right. Now you're experiencing manga as it was meant to be.